*Praise for* **THE WHY**

"PROFOUND . . . A cosmic guide
—*Orlando Sentinel*

"He (Strelecky) has put his finger on the pulse of the world."
—Gannett Media (*USA TODAY . . .*)

"This little book will SURPRISE and INSPIRE readers everywhere. A fable about the opportunities found at emotional crossroads, it says some very important and profound things about life. I highly recommend it."
—Bill Bridges, AUTHOR OF
*TRANSITIONS AND MANAGING TRANSITIONS*

"A simple and LIFE TRANSFORMING story that will change the way you think of life."
—Spirit Works Book Review

"*The Alchemist* for the 21st century."
—*RBA LIBROS, SPAIN*

"LOVED IT!—Read it in one sitting in a day.—LOVED IT! *The Why Café* is DEFINITELY worth a stop."
—*HORIZONS MAGAZINE*

"ORIGINAL . . . IMAGINATIVE . . . COMPELLING
. . . AND LIFE-TRANSFORMING. I ordered ten more

copies of the book before I even finished reading it!"
> —Bill Guggenheim, AUTHOR OF *HELLO FROM HEAVEN*

"Moving, urging, enlightening, insightful . . . UNLOCKS THE ANSWERS TO LIFE'S MOST PRESSING QUESTIONS."
> —*LIFESTYLE MAGAZINE*

"An INSIGHTFUL, INSPIRING READ . . . the characters are extraordinary."
> —*NIGHTS AND WEEKENDS BOOK REVIEW*

"EXCELLENT BOOK to get you to really think about your life and who you really are."
> —Van K. Tharp, BEST-SELLING AUTHOR OF *SAFE STRATEGIES FOR FINANCIAL FREEDOM*

"Once you get into this book YOU WON'T WANT TO PUT IT DOWN!"
> —*MIDWEST BOOK REVIEW*

"ASKS PROFOUND QUESTIONS about the purpose of life and our role as individuals."
> —*PUBLISHERS WEEKLY*

# THE WHY CAFÉ

*Other Works by* **John P. Strelecky**

Life Safari

The Big Five for Life—Leadership's Greatest Secret

How to be Rich and Happy (Coauthor)

Big Five for Life™ (CD Series)

# THE
# WHY
## CAFÉ

∾

## JOHN P. STRELECKY

**Aspen Light Publishing**

Publication Data

Strelecky, John P.
    The Why Café / John P. Strelecky. — 1st Aspen Light Publishing ed.
        p.    cm.
    ISBN-13: 978-0-9743-6206-9 (paperback)


Aspen Light Publishing edition 2011
Da Capo Press edition 2006
First published in 2003 as *The Why Are You Here Café*

Published by Aspen Light Publishing

Inquiries to the publisher can be directed to:
Aspen Light Publishing
13506 Summerport Village Parkway Suite #155
Windermere, FL 34786

The author can be reached through
www.bigfiveforlife.com

2 3 4 5 6 7 8 9

*For Xin, my soul mate in all I do*

*To Sophia, for making my heart smile*

*And to Casey, Mike, and Anne*

A special thanks to Doris S. Michaels and Delia Berrigan Fakis of the DSM Literary Agency for helping people worldwide discover *The Why Café*.

# ∽ **Preface**

Sometimes when you least expect it, and perhaps most need it, you find yourself in a new place, with new people, and you learn new things. That happened to me one night on a dark, lonely stretch of road. In retrospect, my situation at that moment was symbolic of my life at that time. Just as I was lost on the road, I was lost in life as well—unsure of exactly where I was going or why I was moving in that direction.

I'd taken a week off from my job. My goal was to get away from everything associated with work. It wasn't that my job was terrible. Sure, it had its frustrating aspects. More than anything though was that most days I found myself wondering if there wasn't supposed to be more to life than spending ten to twelve hours per day working in a cubicle. The main point of which appeared to be a potential promotion to then work twelve to fourteen hours per day in an office.

During high school I'd prepared for college. In college I'd prepared for the work world. Since then I'd spent my time working my way up in the company where I was employed. Now I was questioning whether the people who helped direct me along those paths were simply repeating to me what someone had repeated to them in their lives.

It wasn't bad advice really, but it wasn't particularly fulfilling advice either. I felt like I was busy trading my life for money, and it didn't seem like such a good trade. That befuddled state of mind is where I was mentally when I found "The Why Are You Here Café."

When I've related this story to others, they've used terms like "mystical" and "Twilight Zone-ish." The latter a reference to an old television program where people would show up in places that at first glance seemed normal, but didn't always end up that way. Sometimes, just for an instant, I catch myself wondering if my experience was real. When that happens, I go into my desk drawer at home and read the inscription on the menu

Casey gave me. It reminds me of just how real everything was.

I've never tried to retrace my steps and find the café again. Some small part of me likes to believe no matter how real the evening was, even if I could go back to the exact spot where I originally found the café, it wouldn't be there—that the only reason I found it was because at that moment, on that night, I needed to find it, and for that reason alone it existed.

Maybe someday I will try to go back. Or maybe some night I'll just find myself in front of it again. Then I can go inside and tell Casey, Mike, and Anne, if she is there, how that night in the café changed my life. How the questions they exposed me to have resulted in thoughts and discoveries beyond anything I'd imagined before then.

Who knows. Perhaps on that night I'll spend the evening talking to someone else who also got lost and wandered into "The Why Café."

Or maybe I'll just write a book about my experience, and let that be part of my contribution to what the café is all about.

## ∽ One

I was creeping along the interstate at a pace that made walking look like a high speed car race. After an hour of slowly inching along, the traffic came to a complete standstill. I hit the scan button on the radio and searched for any sign of intelligent life. There was nothing.

When twenty minutes passed without anyone moving forward, people started to get out of their cars. This didn't actually accomplish anything, but now all of us could complain to someone outside of our own automobile, which was a nice change of pace.

The owner of the minivan in front of me kept repeating that his reservation was going to be cancelled if he didn't get to his hotel by 6:00. The woman in the convertible on my left was on her cell phone, complaining to someone about the inefficiencies of the entire road-way system. Behind me, a carload of youth league base-ball players was driving their chaperone to the brink of her sanity. I could almost hear the woman thinking that this was the last time she ever volunteered for any-thing. Basically, I was a small piece of one long ribbon of discontent.

Finally, after another twenty-five minutes without any signs of forward movement, a police car came driv-ing down the grass center median. Every few hundred feet the car would stop, presumably to let people know what was going on.

"For the sake of that officer," I thought to myself, "I hope they carry riot gear."

With eager anticipation, we all awaited our turn. When the officer finally arrived at our section of the highway, she told us a tanker with potentially toxic materials had overturned about five miles ahead. The road was completely shut down. She explained that our options were to turn around and try an alternate route—although there really wasn't one—or to wait out the cleanup efforts. Those would probably take another hour.

I watched the officer move down to the next group of disconsolate drivers. When the guy with the minivan once again repeated his concerns over his 6:00 reservation, I decided my patience had run out.

"This is exactly the kind of thing that always seems to happen when I'm trying to get away for a while," I mumbled to myself.

I explained to my new friends, who were friends in the childhood way, based primarily on proximity, that I had reached my frustration limit and was going to try a different way. After one final comment about his 6:00 reservation, the minivan owner cleared a path for me, and I crossed the grass median. Then I began heading in a new direction.

## ൭ **Two**

Before leaving on my trip, I'd printed out my driving directions from the Internet. At the time, this seemed super-intelligent. "No need for a map," I thought. "All I have to do is follow these simple, straightforward directions."

Since those were now useless, I turned on my phone and pulled up the map feature it offered. "System unavailable," was all that kept showing on the screen. I longed for the road atlas that used to accompany me on all driving trips.

As I headed south, knowing I should be heading north, my frustration built. Five miles without an exit became ten, then twenty, then twenty-five miles.

"And by the time I find an exit it won't really matter, since I have no idea how to get where I want to go," I said out loud to myself, demonstrating my further degenerating state of mind.

Finally, at mile twenty-eight, an exit appeared.

"This just isn't possible," I thought to myself as I pulled to the top of the exit ramp. "I'm at the one place in probably the entire world that doesn't have a gas station, a fast-food restaurant, or anything else, at a highway intersection." I looked to my left. There was nothing. The view to the right was equally empty.

"Well," I said, "it doesn't look like it matters which way I go."

I turned right, mentally noting I was now going west, and at the next promising intersection I should turn right again. That way, I would at least be heading back north. The road was two lanes, one taking me farther from where I had come, the other taking me back. I really wasn't sure which one I should be on. Traffic was very light. Signs of civilization were even lighter. I saw an occasional house, some family farms, and then nothing but woods and grassland.

An hour later I was officially lost. The only intersections I'd passed were small and marked with the type of signs that immediately indicate you are in trouble. When you haven't seen another person for forty miles, and the road you are on has a name that starts with the word "Old," as in "Old Route 65," things are looking pretty bleak.

At the next intersection, which was really no more major than any of the other intersections I'd driven by, I turned right. It was an act of desperation. At least I would be going in the right compass direction, even if I had no idea where I was. To my dismay, the name of this road also started with "Old."

It was approaching 8:00 P.M., and the sun was sinking lower on the horizon. As the day wound down, my frustration continued to rise.

"I should have just stayed on the expressway," I said in anger. "I was so upset about losing an hour, and now I've wasted two, and still have no idea where the hell I am."

I punched the roof of my car, as if the car had anything to do with the situation, or as if that would help.

Ten, fifteen, twenty more miles, and there was still nothing. I now had less than half a tank of gas. As far as I could tell, going back was no longer an option. With my remaining fuel, I couldn't return to where I'd started, assuming I could even find that place. Even if I made it back, there hadn't been a gas station along the entire route anyway.

My only choice was to plod on and hope I finally found someplace where I could fill up and get some food. My frustration level continued to go in the opposite direction of the fuel gauge.

I was on the trip to avoid frustration. I had plenty of that back home with my job, bills, and, to some degree, with life in general. I didn't need it here, too. This was supposed to be my chance to relax and "recharge my batteries."

"What an odd phrase," I thought to myself. "Recharge my batteries." "Burn out, recharge, burn out, recharge . . . how is that moving in a positive direction?"

The sun had now sunk completely below the tree line and dusk was steadily enveloping the countryside. Traces of pink and orange on the clouds reflected the last essence of daylight, although I barely noticed the sky as I focused on the road and my worsening situation. There was still no sign of any people.

I glanced down at the gas gauge again. "Less than a quarter tank and falling," I said out loud.

The last time I'd slept in my car was driving back from college. That was years ago and I hadn't really planned on re-creating the event. Unfortunately, it looked like that was becoming more and more likely.

"I'll need my sleep," I thought, "so I'll have enough strength to walk for help once the car runs out of gas."

## ⤳ Three

It was when the needle on the fuel gauge just started to slip below the red line with the E on top that I saw the light. Seized by the stupidity of my situation, I had taken a left turn at an intersection a few miles back. There was no indication that my chances of finding anyone were going to be better by taking that turn, but I did it anyway. It was at least a road whose name didn't start with the word "Old," had been my justification at the time.

"An act of desperation that apparently might pay off," I said out loud.

As I got closer to the light, I could see it was a streetlight. A single, white streetlight, shining brightly in a location so remote that it was in the *middle* of the middle of nowhere.

"Please be something there," I repeated in mantra-like fashion as I drove the quarter of a mile toward it. And sure enough, there was something.

At the light, I pulled off the road and into a dirt and gravel parking lot. To my amazement, in front of me was a small, white, rectangular building with the name The Why Are You Here Café spelled out in light-blue neon on the roof. Equally surprising were the three other cars in the parking lot. "Wherever they came from, it must not be from the same place I did," I thought, since I hadn't seen anyone for at least the last hour of my drive. "Which could be good. Hopefully they know something I don't about how to get out of wherever it is I am."

I climbed out of the car and stretched my arms over my head a few times to clear the stiffness from my body. Then I walked toward the entrance. The sky was black, except for a large crescent moon and thousands of stars. As I opened the door to the café, small bells attached to the inner doorknob announced my arrival.

To my surprise, a wave of appetizing smells washed over me. I hadn't realized just how hungry I was until right then. I couldn't place exactly what was generating the aroma, but I planned on ordering three servings of whatever it was.

## ∽ Four

Inside, the café had the feel of an old diner. Chrome-colored soda fountain stools, with red cushioned tops, were lined up under a long, thin, white counter. Under the front windows was a row of red booths, with a table between each section. Every table had a glass container of sugar, a small silver pitcher of what I assumed was milk for coffee, and matching salt and pepper shakers.

An old cash register sat on a stand near the door and next to it was a wooden coat rack. The café felt comfortable. It was the kind of place where you could sit and talk for a long time with friends. Unfortunately, I hadn't brought any of those with me.

A waitress stopped talking to a couple in one of the far booths. She smiled at me and said, "Open seating, park it where you want it."

I did my best to calm the still-simmering frustrations that had built up over the last four hours and attempted to smile back. Then I chose a booth near the door. As I slid onto the red vinyl seat, I noticed how new it looked. I looked around and was surprised at how new everything looked.

"The owner must be anticipating some huge urban growth," I thought, "to build a new café out here in the middle of nowhere."

"Hi there," interrupted my deep thoughts on inexpensive real estate prices and housing development opportunities. It was the waitress. "My name's Casey. How are you?"

"Hi, Casey. I'm John, and I'm a little lost."

"Yes you are, John," she replied with a mischievous smile.

From the way she said it, I couldn't tell if she was affirming that I was John, or that I was lost.

"Why are you here, John?" she asked.

"Well, I was going along and ran into some problems. When I tried to work my way around them, I ended up getting pretty lost. In the process I just about ran out of gas and almost starved to death." Casey smiled her same mischievous smile as I finished my diatribe of frustration.

"I'll tell you what," she said. "I'm sure we can help you avoid the starvation problem. As far as the rest is concerned, we'll just have to see."

She took a menu from the holder by the front door and handed it to me. I wasn't sure if it was the light, or my fatigue from driving for so long, but I could have sworn the letters on the front of the menu dissolved and reappeared as she handed it to me. "I must be really tired," I thought, as I set the menu down on the table.

Casey pulled a small order pad out of her pocket. "Why don't I get you something to drink while you look at the menu," she said. I ordered a glass of water with lemon, and she left to get it for me.

This day was shaping up to be much more than I'd bargained for. First a multi-hour drive through the middle of nothing, then a café on the edge of nowhere, and now a waitress with a mischievous smile. I picked up the menu from the table and read the front cover.

"Welcome to The Why Are You Here Café" was on the top half of the page. Underneath, in small black letters, it said, "Prior to ordering, please consult with our wait staff about what your time here could mean."

"I hope it means I'll be getting something good to eat," I thought to myself as I flipped open the front cover.

Inside, the menu contained the usual assortment of café food. Breakfast items were listed on the left near the top; sandwiches were on the bottom left; appetizers and salads were on the upper right, and entrees were below that. The surprise came when I turned the menu over. On the back cover were three questions under the heading Items to Ponder While You Wait:

*Why are you here?*

*Do you fear death?*

*Are you fulfilled?*

"Not exactly like a glance through the sports pages," I thought to myself. I was about to reread the three questions when Casey came back with my water.

"Finding everything all right?" she asked.

I turned the menu over to the front and pointed to the name of the café.

"What does it mean?"

"Oh, everyone seems to have their own interpretation of that," she replied. "As a matter of fact, most of us here just call it 'The Why Café' for short. Now, what can I get for you?"

I wasn't ready to order. I was a little tempted to reach for my jacket and leave, but I wasn't ready to order yet. There was definitely something different about this place, and I wasn't convinced it was different in a good sort of way. "Sorry, Casey, I'm going to need a little bit longer."

"That's all right," she replied. "You take your time, and I'll come see how you're doing in a few minutes. And John," she said with a smile, "don't worry. You're in good hands here."

## ᦇᦂ Five

I watched as Casey went over to the couple in the booth at the other end of the café. When she arrived, the three of them started to talk. Whatever it was they were discussing must have been good, because all three were smiling and laughing.

"Maybe this place isn't all that bad," I thought. "Perhaps I should have some of whatever they're having."

I turned my attention back to the menu. "There are no other options," I thought to myself. "I'm about out of gas, there appears to be no food anywhere within a two-hundred-mile radius, and although this place seems a little odd, nothing too unusual has actually happened yet."

This eased my concerns a little. When Casey went to the kitchen and then returned, walking past my booth carrying two pieces of strawberry-rhubarb pie, my concerns evaporated even further. I love strawberry-rhubarb pie, and it had been years since I'd had any. I figured if they were making that here, maybe it was a sign of some kind that I should stick around for a while.

Strange questions aside, the items on the menu looked good. I decided on the breakfast platter, even though the standard breakfast hours had ended long ago. Casey was still talking to the couple, so with my decision made, I turned the menu over to the back.

*Why are you here?*

It seemed like a strange question to ask a restaurant customer. Shouldn't you know why someone is in your restaurant? Shouldn't people eating at the restaurant know why they are there? I wasn't sure I understood the question.

*Why are you here?*

Casey's return broke me out of my thought processes.

"Are you ready?" she asked.

I was about to reply yes, but then I remembered the message from the front of the menu about consulting with the wait staff prior to ordering. "I think so," I said and then pointed at the message. "What exactly do I need to ask you about?"

"Oh that," she replied, and smiled again.

I was getting to really like it when she smiled.

"Over the years we've noticed people seem to feel different after they spend some time here," she said. "So now we try to ease them into the whole 'Why are you here?' experience. We share with them a little of what they might expect, in case they aren't quite ready for what they originally thought they could handle."

At this point I was totally confused. Was she talking about food, the café itself, or something completely different?

"If you'd like," she said, "I can bring your order to the cook and get his opinion on what might be best."

"Sure," I replied, feeling even more confused. "I guess so. I'll take the breakfast platter. I know it isn't breakfast time any more, but is it still alright to order that?"

"Is that what you want?" she asked.

"Yes, it is."

"Then I'm sure it won't be a problem. After all, it's closer to breakfast tomorrow than to lunch today."

I glanced at my watch. It was 10:30 P.M. "That's an interesting way to look at it," I said.

Casey smiled, "Sometimes it helps to look at things from a different perspective."

She wrote down my order and turned away. I watched her walk toward the kitchen and then noticed she'd left the menu on the table.

## ∞ Six

As Casey approached the order window, I saw for the first time that there was a man in the kitchen. He had a wooden serving spoon in one hand and was obviously the person in charge of the cooking. When Casey reached the window, she said something to him. He looked out at me and saw I was looking in his direction. Then he smiled and waved.

I waved back, feeling a little ridiculous. I don't make a habit of waving to cooks in cafés. Casey and the man talked for a few minutes, then she put my order onto the small circular ticket holder and walked back to my table. The man spun the holder until the ticket was in front of him, looked at it for a moment, and then took it back into the kitchen.

I returned my focus to the back of the menu. As I reread the first question—"*Why are you here?*"—Casey came back and sat in the booth across from me.

"That's Mike," she said. "He owns this place and does all the cooking. He said he'll come out and meet you when he has a chance. I asked him about your order, and he said it will be a lot, but he thinks you can handle it."

"That's some kind of service."

She smiled, "We think so. Going back to this," she said and pointed to the front of the menu where it referred to asking the wait staff. "It relates to the question you keep reading on the back of the menu."

I wasn't sure how she knew I'd been reading the question, but I didn't reply.

"You see," she said, "it's one thing to look at that question. It's another to change it."

"What do you mean?"

"It sounds simple, as if it would have no impact," she replied. "But if you modify just a few letters in that question, it changes things."

I looked at her, confused. "Changes things? What types of things? Like I won't be able to eat here, or I'll have to order something different?"

"No," she said, suddenly getting more serious, "bigger changes."

I definitely didn't follow where she was going with this, but she was obviously not kidding. "I'm not sure I understand."

Casey pointed to the menu again. "If you change the question to no longer be something you ask someone else, but instead you change it to something you ask yourself—you'll no longer be the same person."

I was stunned. No longer be the same person? What did that mean? Suddenly I had the sensation of being on the edge of a large cliff. And I wasn't sure if she was explaining to me that taking one step forward would bring immediate death or eternal happiness.

"It's kind of like that," she said, and smiled, "but not so drastic."

Before I could ask how she knew what I was thinking, she continued. "Let me show you without you having to take the step. Read the first question on the menu, but read it in the detached way you might glance at a sign as you walk past it."

I briefly looked down at the menu. To my surprise, the question was no longer *"Why are you here?"*

It now read, *"Why am I here?"*

As soon as I finished reading it, the question changed back to *"Why are you here?"*

"What happened?" I exclaimed. "Did the menu just change? How did you do that?"

"John, I'm not sure if you're ready for the answer to that."

"What do you mean? How did you do it, how did you make the menu change?" By now I was totally confused with what was going on and not all that sure I wanted to stick around and figure it out. Casey recaptured my attention with a question.

"John, did you see what the text on the menu turned into?"

"Sure, it was one thing when I read it the first time, and then it changed back to what it is now. Why? And how did that happen?"

Casey turned the menu over to the front, and pointed to the bottom where the "Prior to ordering . . . " message was printed. "It's like this, John," she began.

"The question that you saw, the one that was different—"

"The one that said, 'Why am I here?'" I interrupted.

"Yes, that one. It's not a question to be taken lightly. To glance at it is one thing. But when you go beyond glancing and actually see it, and then truly ask it of

yourself—your world changes. I know that sounds drastic, and that's why we put the message on the front of
the menu."

## ೦ഌ **Seven**

I was struck by how ludicrous my whole situation seemed. I was in a café, in the middle of the night, in the middle of nowhere, hearing about messages put on the front of menus to help customers deal with their *worlds changing*.

Not exactly a typical start to a vacation. Little did I know this was just the beginning of what the evening held in store for me.

Casey looked at me, "You see John, once you truly ask the question you saw, seeking the answer will become part of your being. You'll find yourself waking up with the question first thing in the morning, and having it constantly flash through your mind during the day. Although you may not remember it, you'll be thinking about it while you sleep, too. It's a little like a gateway. Once you open it up, it beckons you. And once open, it's very hard to close."

I was beginning to realize the *"Why are you here?"* question on the menu had a much deeper meaning than I'd thought when I first read it. From the way Casey was speaking, it was clear it wasn't just asking why someone was in the café.

"That's correct," said Casey, interrupting my thoughts. "It's not about the café. It's asking why someone exists *at all.*"

I sat back in my booth and looked around, feeling stunned. "What kind of place is this?" I wondered.

I tried to gather my thoughts. "Listen Casey, I just came here for some food. All this stuff you're talking about sounds very ominous. I mean, if what you just said about gateways and things constantly flashing through your mind each day is true, I'm not sure why anyone would ever ask themselves that question. I've never asked it and I'm fine."

Casey put the menu on the table. "Are you?" she asked. "Are you really *fine*?" She said the word "fine" with a friendly bit of mockery, as if teasing me to define it. "Many people are *fine*. But some seek something more fulfilling than fine, something greater."

"And so they come to The Why Café?" I asked sarcastically.

"Some of them do," she said in a soft, calm voice. "Is that why you're here?"

I was taken aback. I didn't know how to answer her question. I wasn't sure what I was doing here. I wasn't even sure I knew what this place was.

If I were totally honest with myself, I'd admit that for years I'd wondered if there wasn't more to life than what I already knew about. It wasn't that life was bad. Sure it was frustrating at times, particularly lately, but I had a decent job and good friends. Life *was* fine, even good. Still, in the back of my mind was this feeling I couldn't quite explain.

"That feeling is what inspires people to ask the question you saw," Casey said.

I was shocked. Not just that she seemed to have read my thoughts again, although that alone was very disconcerting. I was shocked by the realization she might be right. I took a long, slow breath. It felt like I was on the edge of that cliff again. I took a half step forward.

"Casey, can you tell me more about the question?"

She nodded, "As I said earlier, asking it opens up a gateway of sorts. The person's mind, soul, or however you view it, will want to seek out the answer. The question will be at the forefront of the person's existence until they figure it out."

"Are you saying that once someone asks themselves 'Why am I here?' they won't be able to ignore the question?" I asked.

"No, it's not that they won't be able to. Some people glance at it, and perhaps even see it, and then they forget about it. But for those individuals who ask the question, and on some level truly want to know the answer, ignoring it becomes very difficult."

"Suppose someone asks the question and then finds the answer," I asked. "What then?"

"Well, that's the good news and the challenging news," she replied, and smiled.

"As I mentioned, asking the question creates the drive to seek out the answer.

"Once someone finds the answer, an equally powerful force emerges. You see, once a person knows why they are here, why they exist, their reason for being alive—they'll want to fulfill that reason. It's like knowing where the X is on a treasure map. Once you've seen the X, it's harder to ignore the treasure. It's harder to not go after it. In this case, once someone knows why they are here, it will be emotionally and even physically more difficult to not fulfill that reason."

I sat back in my chair, trying to process all that Casey was explaining. "So it could actually make things worse," I replied. "Like I said before, a person might be better off never asking the question. They could just go on as they have been and keep the genie in the bottle, so to speak."

Casey looked at me, "Some people choose that. It's something each person, when they get to that point, must decide for him or herself."

I wasn't sure what to do or say. I laughed nervously, remembering how excited I 'd been to finally see the light when I was lost. Now I didn't know what to think.

"This is a lot to be confronted with," I said.

"I hope not 'confronted with,' but more like 'exposed to,'" replied Casey. "You know that feeling you described earlier? It isn't something you can be told or have dictated to you, and if at any time you decide to walk away from it, the choice will be yours and only yours."

With that, she got up from the table, "Speaking of walking away, I'm going to go see how your breakfast special is doing."

I'd totally forgotten about the food I ordered. Now that she reminded me, I was slowly brought back to the realization I was still in a café and still starving.

## ↷ **Eight**

My mind was spinning. I looked down at the menu and re-read the first question.

*Why are you here?*

It had a whole different meaning now compared to the first time I'd read it. I tried to remember the exact words Casey used earlier . . . "It's asking why someone exists at all."

On a level I couldn't quite explain, I felt like something was pulling me to ask the question I'd briefly seen on the menu when I was talking with Casey. I remembered what it was.

*Why am I here?*

I also remembered Casey's comments on the ramifications that might come about from truly asking it.

"This is crazy," I said to myself, and rubbed my eyes. "All I need is some food, a little gasoline, and a place to crash for a few hours. What am I doing thinking about all of these other things?"

I drank half of my water, and as I put down the glass, I noticed Mike was standing next to the table with a pitcher.

"Can I give you a refill?" he asked. "You look like you might be able to handle a little more."

I accepted his offer and he filled the clear tumbler.

"My name is Mike," he said.

I stood up and we shook hands. "Nice to meet you Mike, I'm John."

"Are you okay, John? It seemed like you were pretty deep in thought when I walked over."

"Something like that," I replied, and sat back down. "Casey was explaining to me what the text on the front of the menu means. I'm still trying to sort it out and see if it means anything for me."

As I finished speaking, I realized Mike might not have any idea what Casey and I had been talking about. Even though he was the owner, maybe she was the one who had come up with the questions on the menu and the text on the cover. He didn't hesitate for a second, though.

"Yeah, that's a tough one. People face it at all different times. Some sort it out when they're little kids, some when they're older, and other people never do. It's funny that way."

Since Mike seemed to understand the path Casey and I had started walking with our conversations, I decided to ask him the question that was on my mind.

"Mike, Casey explained to me what some of the ramifications are if someone asks themselves a personal version of this question," I said, and pointed toward the menu. "But I was wondering what they do after that?"

Mike glanced at the menu. "Do you mean after they ask the question, or after they find out the answer?"

I paused for a few seconds while I thought through his question. "Both, I guess. We didn't go into too many details about how someone actually finds out the answer, or what they do once they know. She just explained to me a little about what it would be like once they did know."

"Well, as far as how to find the answer, I don't think there is just one method that works for every person. We all approach life in our own way. I can tell you some of the techniques used by the people I know who have found their answer."

I was about to reply, but caught myself and paused for a moment. I had a hunch that having some insight into how to find the answer to the question might make it even harder not to ask it.

"That's true," said Mike. "Same theory as Casey probably explained to you."

I was only moderately surprised that he, too, seemed to know what I was thinking before I said it out loud.

I wasn't sure I wanted to learn what other people had done. After all, I wasn't even sure I wanted to ask the question yet.

"Mike, what about the other piece? What does someone do once they know the answer to the question?"

Mike smiled. "I'll tell you what, why don't I go check on your order, and when I come back I'll answer that."

A few moments later he returned with a tray full of plates. "Is that all mine?" I asked, wondering what two paragraphs of description about my food I hadn't read on the menu.

"Absolutely. One breakfast platter, complete with omelet, toast, ham, bacon, fresh fruit, hash browns, biscuits, and a side of pancakes."

I looked around to see if there were three other people interested in joining me.

"In addition to that, we've got jelly for the toast, syrup for the pancakes, honey for the biscuits, and our special tomato salsa for the omelet. I'm glad you're hungry."

"I'm not sure anyone is this hungry," I said.

"You'd be surprised, John. Sometimes you just don't know how ready you are for something filling."

Mike put the food on the table. "John, I need to go talk with the couple at the other side of the café for a little bit, but I'll come back and we can continue our conversation then if that's okay with you."

"Sure," I replied, as I looked at all the plates in front of me, "no problem."

## ∾ **Nine**

I began to tackle my table of food. As I was making progress on the omelet, toast, and fruit, Casey came by.

"How are you doing, John?"

I finished chewing the bite I had just put in my mouth. "I'm good, really good. The food is excellent."

"You seem in better spirits."

I was in better spirits. The frustration that was overwhelming me when I came into the café had almost entirely disappeared. I'd gotten so focused on the *"Why are you here?"* question and the ensuing discussions, that everything else had become secondary. The presence of a great-tasting omelet hadn't hurt, either.

"Would you like to finish your meal alone, or do you prefer to have company?" Casey asked.

"Company, definitely company. As a matter of fact, I'd like to continue the discussion we were having earlier. I've been thinking about it and I'm still a little confused regarding some things."

"What can I clarify for you?" Casey asked.

"Well, it's about the question on the menu. When someone asks themselves why they are here, and they somehow figure out the reason, what do they do with that knowledge?"

Casey paused for a few moments. "First of all, they can do whatever they want with it. They uncovered it, and it belongs to them. They have ultimate and total say about what to do."

I thought about her comments for a moment. "I suppose if someone figured out the reason they're here, they would want to figure out the best way to fulfill that reason. The question is, how do they do that?" I looked at Casey and got the impression she knew something but was waiting for me to figure it out on my own.

"It's an individual thing," she said.

I looked at her. "How about a hint?"

"Perhaps an example would be helpful," she replied. "Suppose you wanted to become an artist in your spare time, what type of art would you create?"

I thought for a moment. "I don't know. I suppose it would depend on what type of artist I wanted to be. I guess I would just create whatever I wanted." I stopped and waited for her to comment. She didn't, so I thought through my answer.

"Is it that simple?" I asked. "Once someone knows why they are here, they do whatever they want that fulfills their reason?"

As I said the words, I felt a sense of excitement race through my body. It was like I had just found something out that was unique and important, and my body was confirming it. It sounded so basic that it was almost too basic to be right. *Do whatever you want that fulfills the reason why you are here.*

"So if the reason I'm here is to help people, then I should do whatever I want that fits my definition of helping people?" I asked excitedly, warming to the concept.

"That's correct," said Casey. "If helping people to you means joining the medical profession, you should do that. If it means building shelters in an impoverished area, then do that. Perhaps you feel becoming an accountant and assisting people with their taxes is the way you want to help. Then you should do that."

My mind was spinning. I had never really thought of things in this context before. Much of my life had been spent making decisions in response to other reasons, like family advice, cultural pressures, and people's opinions. This was something different. "So what if I'm here to experience what it's like to be a millionaire?"

"Then you should do whatever fits your definition of 'be a millionaire,'" she replied. "If that means interacting with millionaires, do that. If it means working until you have a million dollars, do that. Just like in the other examples, the choice is always yours."

"'Be a millionaire' . . . I kind of like the sound of that," I said, getting more and more excited. "I could buy a few new cars, maybe a couple of houses." Casey's voice became quiet.

"Is that why you are here?"

Her question caused my mind to stop racing.

"I don't know."

"Mike and I have a little acronym we use," she said. "It relates to the question you saw briefly on the menu."

I looked down and read the first question.

*Why are you here?*

"When a person knows the reason they are here, they have identified their 'Purpose For Existing.' We call it 'PFE' for short. During someone's lifetime, they may find they want to do ten, twenty, or hundreds of things to fulfill their Purpose For Existing. They can do all of them. Our most fulfilled customers are the ones who know their PFE, and try all the activities they believe will fulfill it."

"And your least fulfilled customers?" I asked.

"They do lots of things, too," she said.

She paused, and I spoke the thought that leapt into my mind. "They do lots of things that aren't part of their PFE." Casey smiled, and I realized this was one of those conclusions I needed to arrive at on my own.

"Casey, if I asked myself the question, and eventually figured out my Purpose For Existing, how would I learn what could help me fulfill it? I mean it might be people, traveling, activities, experiences, or all kinds of things. It seems a little overwhelming."

She replied with a question. I was beginning to notice she often replied with a question. "John, suppose you determine your Purpose For Existing is to know how to build cars, and you decide you want to fulfill that PFE. What would you do?"

I thought for a moment. "I suppose I would read lots of books about cars. Maybe I'd visit a place where they build cars, or contact some people who had built cars and get their advice. I might try to get a job where I assemble cars."

"Would you stay in one place?"

I paused and thought again. "No, I suppose if I really wanted to know how to build cars, I'd visit different places in the world where they did that, so I wouldn't know just one way. I guess, to answer my own question, a person learns about all the things that could fulfill their Purpose For Existing by exploring and getting exposure to a lot of things related to their PFE."

"You've got it," Casey said. "We are all limited by our current experiences and knowledge. The important word there is 'current.' More than ever before in the history of the world as we know it, we each have the chance to gain exposure to information, people, cultures, and experiences from all over the world."

Casey continued, "As we try to find what will fulfill our PFE, our limits today are much less about accessibility, and much more about limitations we impose on ourselves."

"You're right," I said. "And yet it seems like I don't take advantage of that accessibility very much. When I think of the way I spend my time, it's pretty much the same thing each day."

"Why is that?" she asked.

I looked down at the menu.

*Why are you here?*

"I guess maybe it's because I don't know the answer to this question," I said and pointed at the menu. "Without knowing exactly why I am here, and what I want to do, I just do the things most people are doing."

"In your experience, does doing what 'most people' are doing help you fulfill your Purpose For Existing?" she asked.

## ॐ **Ten**

Casey's question had my mind racing. Does doing what most people are doing help me fulfill my Purpose For Existing? Before I could answer, she spoke again.

"Have you ever seen a green sea turtle, John?"

"A sea turtle?"

"Correct," Casey said, "a sea turtle. In particular, a big green sea turtle, with green splotches on its flippers and head."

"I suppose I've seen pictures of one," I said. "Why?"

"As strange as it may sound," Casey began, "I learned one of my most important life lessons about choosing what things to do each day from a big green sea turtle."

"What did he tell you?" I asked, not at all successful in suppressing my smile.

"Funny," she answered, and smiled back. "He didn't specifically 'tell' me anything, but he taught me a great deal just the same. I was snorkeling off the coast of Hawaii. The day had already been spectacular, in that I had seen a purple spotted eel and an octopus, both of which were new for me. There were also thousands and thousands of fish, representing every color you can imagine, from the most striking neon blue to the deepest shades of red.

"I was about 100 feet away from the beach, and diving down among some large rock structures, when I turned to my right and saw a large green sea turtle swimming next to me. That was the first time I'd ever seen one in the wild, so I was ecstatic. I rose to the surface, cleared my snorkel, and floated on top of the water, so I could watch him.

"He was right underneath me when I looked down, and he was swimming away from the shore. I decided I would stay on the surface and just watch him for a while. To my surprise, although he appeared to be moving pretty slowly, sometimes paddling his flippers and other times just floating in the water, I couldn't keep up with him. I was wearing fins, which gave me propulsion power through the water, and didn't have on a buoyancy vest or anything that would slow me down, and yet he kept moving farther from me even though I was trying to keep up.

"After about ten minutes, he lost me. Tired, disappointed, and a little embarrassed that I couldn't keep up with a turtle, I turned back toward the beach and snorkeled to shore.

"The next day I returned to the same spot, with the hope of seeing more turtles. Sure enough, about thirty minutes after walking into the water, I turned to look at a school of tiny black and yellow fish, and there was another green sea turtle. I watched him for a while as he paddled around the coral. Then I tried to follow him as he swam away from the shore. Once again, I was surprised to find I couldn't keep up. When I realized he was pulling ahead of me, I stopped paddling and just floated and watched him. It was at that moment when he taught me the important life lesson."

Casey stopped speaking.

"Casey, you can't just end the story there. What did he teach you?"

She smiled at me. "I thought you were a nonbeliever in green sea turtles being able to tell you something?"

I smiled back. "I'm still doubtful on the 'tell' part, but from the way the story is going, I'm starting to become a believer in the teaching possibilities. What happened next?"

"Well, as I was floating on the surface, I realized that the turtle linked its movements to the movements of the water. When a wave was going toward the shore, and in the face of the turtle, he would float, and paddle just enough to hold his position. When the pull of the wave was back out to the ocean, he would paddle faster, so that he was using the movement of the water to his advantage.

"The turtle never fought the waves, but instead he used them. The reason I had not been able to keep up with him was because I was paddling all the time, no matter which way the water was flowing. At first this was fine, and I was able to stay with him. I even had to slow my paddling sometimes. But the more I battled against the incoming waves, the more tired I became. This meant that when the wave was going out, I didn't have enough energy to take advantage of it.

"As wave after wave came in and went out, I became more and more fatigued and less effective. The turtle kept optimizing his movements with the movements of the water, though. That's why he was able to swim faster than I could."

"Casey," I began, "I think I appreciate a good turtle story . . ."

"Green sea turtle story," she interrupted me, and smiled.

"Right, green sea turtle story. I think I appreciate a good green sea turtle story as much as the next person. Probably more, actually, since I love the ocean. I'm not sure I understand how this relates to the way people choose the things that will fill up their days, though."

"And I had such high hopes for you," she said, and smiled again.

"Okay, okay," I replied. "Give me a minute." I thought through what we had been talking about before the green sea turtle story. Then I began speaking again. "You were saying that once someone knows why they are here—they know their PFE—then they can spend their time doing things that fulfill it. You were also saying that people who don't know their PFE also spend their time on lots of things. That's when I deduced that the things they spend their time on are things that *don't* help them fulfill their PFE."

"So far so reflective, and I think I can sense a major insight just around the corner," she said.

"Yes you can," I replied, and smiled at her entertaining sarcasm. "I think the turtle—the green sea turtle—taught you that if you aren't in tune with what you want to do, you can waste your energy on lots of things. Then when opportunities come up to do what you want, you might not have the strength or time to spend on them."

"Very nice," she said. "And I appreciate the catch on the 'green sea turtle' instead of just 'turtle.'" She became more serious. "It was a really big moment for me, definitely one of my 'Aha' moments in life.

"Each day there are so many people trying to persuade you to spend your time and energy on them. Think about your mail. If you were to participate in every activity, sale, and service offering you get notified of, you would have no free time. And that's just the mail. Add on all the people who want to capture your attention for television time, online activities, places to eat, travel destinations. . . . You can quickly find yourself doing what everyone else is doing, or wants you to do.

"When I got back to the beach after watching the turtle on the second day, I was filled with all of these insights. I sat on my towel and wrote them down in my journal. I realized that in my life, the incoming waves are made up of all the people, activities, and things that are trying to capture my attention, energy, and time but are not associated with my PFE. The outgoing waves are the people, activities, and things that can *help me* fulfill my PFE. Therefore, the more time and energy I waste on the incoming waves, the less time and energy I have for the outgoing ones.

"Once I had that picture in my head, it really put things in a different perspective. I became much more selective about how much 'paddling' I did, and for what reasons."

"Interesting," I said, reflecting on her story and how I spent most of my time each day. "I see what you meant by learning something from a green sea turtle."

Casey got up from the table. "I thought you might. However, I think I'm keeping you from eating your breakfast. Why don't I let you work on that for a while,

and I'll come back in a little bit to see how you're doing."

"Casey, can I borrow a piece of paper and your pen
before you go?"

"Sure." She took the pen out of her apron, ripped
off a piece of paper from her order pad, and put both of
them on the table.

"The answer will surprise you," she said with a wink,
as she walked away.

"How do you know—?" I started to ask, but she was
already on her way to the back of the café.

I started writing figures on the paper. Average life ex-
pectancy of seventy-five years . . . twenty-two years old
when I graduated college . . . six days per week that I
receive mail . . . awake sixteen hours per day . . . twenty
minutes each day spent on mail and e-mail. . . .

When I finished all my computing, I couldn't believe
the answer. I did the math again. Same answer.

I realized Casey wasn't kidding about the impact of
the incoming wave. If from the time I graduated college until the time I was seventy-five years old, I spent
twenty minutes per day opening and looking at mail
and e-mail I didn't really care about—that used up almost an entire year of my life.

I rechecked my math a third time. It was true. There were probably fifty-three years of life after college, and if I wasn't careful, I would waste one of them reading junk mail.

"Well?" It was Casey. She had returned from the kitchen, but I was so caught up in my math efforts I didn't notice her.

"You're right," I replied. "I am surprised. Actually, I think I'm beyond surprised and quickly heading to shocked. Do you realize that junk mail alone could eat up an entire year of your life?"

She smiled, "Not all mail and e-mail is junk mail, John."

"No, I know, but at least for me a lot of it is. Besides, it's not just those things. I was sitting here wondering what other incoming wave items are occupying my time and energy every day."

"It can get you thinking," she said. "That's why my time with the green sea turtle made such a big impact on me." She smiled, then turned and walked toward the people at the other end of the café.

## ᘒ **Eleven**

I started working on the pancakes. They were as deli-
cious as the other items had been. As I ate, I thought
about my conversations with Mike and Casey. They
were not your average café conversations. Why are
you here? What do you do once you know why you are
here? What can you learn from a green sea turtle?

As I was making some progress on the rest of the
fruit, Mike came over to my table.

"How's the food, John?"

"Terrific, this is some place. You should think of
franchising, you could make a fortune."

Mike smiled, "Maybe I already have a fortune."

"Then why would you be working here . . . ?" I
stopped myself, already too late. "Sorry Mike, I didn't

mean that this isn't a great place. I just meant . . . I'm not sure what I meant, actually."

"That's okay," said Mike. "I've gotten that question more than once. John, did you ever hear the story of the businessman who went on vacation and met a fisherman?"

"I don't think so."

"It was a popular little story a couple of years ago," said Mike. "Interested? It relates to your comment on franchising."

"Sure," I replied.

"Well, the story goes that a businessman went on vacation to get away from it all, to 'recharge his batteries,' so to speak. He flew to this faraway location and wandered into a small village. Over the course of a few days, he watched the people in the community and noticed there was one fisherman in particular who seemed the happiest and the most content of everyone. The businessman was curious about this, so one day he approached the fisherman and asked him what he did every day.

"The man replied that he woke up every morning and had breakfast with his wife and children. Then his kids would go off to school, he would go fishing, and his wife would paint. He would fish for a few hours, return with enough fish for the family meals, and then he would take a nap. After dinner, he and his wife would take a walk along the beach and watch the sunset while the kids swam in the ocean.

"The businessman was stunned. 'You do this every day?' he asked.

"'Most days,' replied the fisherman. 'Sometimes we do other things, but for the most part, yes, this is my life.'

"'And every day you can catch fish?' asked the businessman.

"'Yes,' replied the fisherman. 'There are many fish.'

"'Can you catch more than just the fish you bring home for your family?' inquired the businessman.

"The fisherman looked at him, smiled, and replied, 'Oh yes, I often catch many more and just let them go. You see, I love fishing.'

"'Well, why don't you fish all day and catch as many as you can?' asked the businessman. 'Then you could sell the fish and make lots of money. Pretty soon you could buy a second boat, and then a third boat, and their fishermen could catch lots of fish, too. In a few years you could have an office in a major city, and I bet within ten years you could have an international fish distribution business.'

"The fisherman smiled again at the businessman. 'Why would I do all that?'

"'Well, for the money,' replied the businessman. 'You would do it so you could get lots of money and then retire.'

"'And what would I do when I retired?' asked the fisherman, still smiling.

"'Well, whatever you want, I suppose,' said the businessman.

"'For instance, maybe I could eat breakfast with my family?'

"'Yes, I guess so,' said the businessman, a little annoyed that the fisherman wasn't more excited about his idea.

"'And if I wanted to, since I love fishing so much, I could fish a little bit each day?' the fisherman continued.

"'I don't see why not,' said the businessman. 'There probably won't be as many fish by then, but there should still be some.'

"'Then perhaps I could spend my evenings with my wife, walking along the beach and watching the sunset, while our children swam in the ocean?' inquired the fisherman.

"'Sure, whatever you want, although by then your kids will probably be grown,' said the businessman.

"The fisherman smiled at the other man, shook his hand, and wished him well on his efforts to recharge."

Mike finished the story and looked at me. "What do you think, John?"

"I think I'm a little bit like the businessman. I spend most of my days working so that I'll have enough money to retire."

"I used to do that, too," said Mike. "But I came to a very important realization for me. Retirement was this time in the future when I would have enough money to do what I wanted. I would be free to participate in the activities I liked, and could spend every day in a way that fulfilled me. Then one evening, after a particularly unfulfilling day at work, I came to the conclusion that there had to be a better way. Over time I learned that somehow I'd gotten confused about how things should work. It was so simple it seemed crazy that I'd gotten it confused, but nonetheless I had."

I continued to eat my food as Mike spoke.

"I realized that for me, every day is an opportunity to do whatever I want. Every day I have a chance to fulfill the answer to the question you glimpsed on the back of the menu. I don't need to wait until 'retirement.'"

I put my fork down and sat back. I was a little surprised at just how simple that sounded. "But that's so easy," I said. "If it's that easy, why doesn't everyone do what they want?"

"Well," replied Mike smiling, "I'm afraid I can't speak for everyone. Are you doing what you want, John?"

This wasn't the direction I expected the conversation to go. I was hoping Mike would keep doing the talking, and I could just listen. I thought about his question for a moment.

"No, not really," I replied.

"Why not?"

This was further progress down a path I hadn't anticipated. "To be honest, I'm not sure. I didn't really know what I wanted to study when I went to college. Eventually I made the decision to go into a program I kind of liked and that a lot of people told me was a good field for getting a job after graduation. When school ended, I started working, and then my focus shifted more and more toward making money. Eventually I was earning a pretty good salary, and I just sort of settled into a pattern.

"I'm also not sure I ever thought about this question," I said, and pointed at the menu. "Not until tonight."

"Like I mentioned earlier," Mike commented, "it's kind of funny how and when it hits different people."

"This really seems crazy," I said.

"What do you mean?"

"What we were just talking about. Why is it that we spend so much of our time preparing for when we can do what we want, instead of just doing what we want right now?"

"I think there's someone you should meet who might be able to provide some insight into that one," Mike said. He got up from the table and went to where Casey was talking with the other customers. I couldn't hear what they were discussing, but in a few moments one of the people got up and began walking toward me.

## ৩ **Twelve**

When they reached the table, Mike introduced me to the woman he had brought over. "John, I'd like you to meet a friend of mine, this is Anne. Anne, this is John. Tonight is his first time at the café."

Anne smiled and we shook hands.

"Nice to meet you," I said. "I take it from Mike's introduction that you dine here at the café a lot."

"Every once in a while," she replied. "It's one of those places you just kind of find yourself at when you need it most."

"I'm beginning to sense that," I said.

"John and I were just discussing one of your favorite topics, Anne, so I thought perhaps we could bring you in for an expert opinion."

She laughed. "Well, I'm not sure about the expert part, but I'm never short of an opinion. What were you talking about?"

"John was asking why we spend so much of our time preparing for when we can do what we want, instead of just doing those things right now."

"Ah, that is one of my favorite topics," she said, and laughed again.

Anne's laugh was infectious, and I liked her immediately. "Please sit down, Anne. I'd like to hear your perspective. You too, Mike, if you can spare the time."

As they slid into the booth across from me, Mike said, "Before she begins, you should know a little about Anne. She has an advanced degree from the top marketing school in the world and was a highly acclaimed executive in the advertising world for many years."

"Wow," I said. "That sounds very impressive."

"Not necessarily," she replied with a smile, "but it's probably important for context. John, do you ever watch television, read magazines, browse the web, or listen to the radio?"

"Sometimes," I said. "Why?"

"Part of the answer to your question about why we spend so much time preparing to do what we want, instead of just doing it, lies in the messages that are placed in front of us every day," she replied. "You see, advertisers have long known that if you effectively target people's fears and their desire to be fulfilled, you can motivate them to do things. If you can play to the right fear, or to the right desire, you can get them to buy specific goods and use particular services."

"Can you give me an example?" I asked.

"Well, have you ever seen or heard an advertisement where the content focused on enabling you to be happy or secure? Something where the message was, 'If you have this product, your life will be better?'"

"I'm not sure," I said. "I suppose so."

"It's usually subtle," she commented. "Most of the time companies don't come right out and say it. But when you know what to look for, or when you've been involved with creating a lot of advertisements, you see it. The purpose of those messages is to get you to believe that you can achieve fulfillment through a particular product or service. For instance, driving this automobile will bring meaning to your life, eating that ice cream will translate into happiness, having this diamond will mean contentment.

"And," she continued, "let me tell you something very important. An even more subtle but more impactful message is usually conveyed. Not only will those products enable you to be fulfilled if you have them, but they can *keep you* from being fulfilled if you don't have them."

I looked at her quizzically. "Anne, are you saying people should never buy anything? That seems pretty extreme, and not very practical either."

"Oh no," she replied. "Don't get me wrong. Each person should do whatever they want. I'm not saying don't buy a car or go to the mall or eat ice cream.

"You asked why we spend so much time preparing for what we want to do instead of just doing it. Part of the answer is if we aren't careful, we buy into the mass of marketing messages we are exposed to every day. We end up believing the answer to happiness and fulfillment lies in a product or service. Eventually that can result in us putting ourselves in a financial position where we feel we have to keep doing something that isn't what we want to do."

"I'm not sure I understand," I said.

"Let me give you a very general example," Anne began. "Keep in mind that this doesn't apply to every person, but it should help explain what we've been talking about.

"From a young age, we are exposed to advertisements conveying the message that fulfillment comes from things. So what do we do? Well naturally, we buy some items to see if the advertisements are true.

"The challenge is," she continued, "that buying those things requires money. To solve that problem, we get a job. It may not be our ideal job, and the time we spend at work may not be exactly how we want to spend the hours of our life, but we take the job so we can pay off the things we bought. We tell ourselves it's temporary. Soon we'll be doing something else, something more in line with what we really want to do.

"The problem is, because the job isn't fulfilling, and because we spend so much time at our job, we feel more and more unfulfilled. Around us are many people who talk about how they can't wait for that day in the future when they will retire and *then* do the things they want to do. Before long, we too start to envision this almost mystical time in the future. The date when we won't have to do our job either, and can instead spend time doing the things we want to do.

"Meanwhile, to offset the fact that we aren't spending every day doing what we want, we purchase some more things. We hope that in some small way the advertising messages are true, and those items will bring the fulfill-ment our daily work life does not. Unfortunately, the more we purchase, the more bills we have, and therefore the more time we need to spend at work so we can pay for everything. Since time at our job is not really the way we want to spend our life, more time at work results in more feelings of unfulfillment because now we have *even less* time for what we want to do."

"And so we buy more things," I said. "I think I see where this is going. It doesn't sound like a very positive cycle."

"Positive or not," replied Anne, "the end result is people keep working for a long time at things that don't necessarily fulfill their PFE. Meanwhile, they keep looking to the future for when they don't have to work anymore, and can finally do what they want."

"Wow, I've never thought of it that way before," I said. "Are you sure about all of this?"

Anne and Mike both laughed. "John, just as I wouldn't recommend taking advertising messages at face value, but for you to see them for what they are, I wouldn't want you to simply accept anything I say," Anne re-plied. "Casey mentioned you were talking about how we all have the chance to expand our exposure to things, and that's how we know what exists. What I've shared with you is just one person's opinion. Now that you've heard it, you can look at the world around you and decide if you think some, all, or none of it is true."

"Well, it's definitely going to make me think about things in a new way," I said. "Tell me, Anne, the example you just gave, did you go through that cycle?"

Anne laughed. "Absolutely. I can laugh about it now, but at the time it wasn't funny. I was really unhappy and felt like I wasn't in control of my own life. Every day I worked long hours, and then tried to make up for my lack of free time by treating myself to things. In my mind this was a very rational approach to life.

"I worked all weekend, I would say to myself, so I deserve a treat of a new outfit, the latest electronic gadget, or some new stylish home furnishing. The problem was, since I was always working, I rarely had time to use what I treated myself to. People would come over to my house and tell me how much they loved it, but I was seldom there enough to enjoy it.

"One night, after I'd gone through a large stack of bills that would once again eat up most of my income for the month, I fell back on my bed and stared up at the ceiling. It was all I could do not to break into tears.

I realized life was passing me by. I was spending it at a job I didn't really care about, and trying to compensate myself by buying things that, in truth, I didn't really care about either.

"To compound the problem, my plan for getting back to doing what I wanted, required me to work until I was sixty years old, when I could retire. It was a miserable feeling."

"That seems like a very different mind-set than you have now," I said. "What happened?"

Anne smiled and replied, "It was a different mind-set. That evening, after staring at the ceiling and trying to figure out how I'd gotten myself to where I was, I decided to go for a walk. I lived in a large city, and the streets were full of people. I kept looking at every person I passed, wondering whether any of them felt the same way I did.

"Were they happy? Were they doing what they wanted to be doing? Were they feeling fulfilled? Eventually, I stopped in a small coffee shop I'd seen a number of times but never visited. To my surprise, an acquaintance of mine was sitting there. I'd met him on a few occasions and was impressed by how at ease he always seemed.

"He asked me to join him, and over three hours and many cups of coffee, we traded theories on life. When I explained my situation to him, he smiled and suggested that maybe I was reading too many of my own advertisements. I told him I wasn't sure what he meant, and so he explained the cycle I described to you earlier. He went on to tell me something else, which has stuck with me ever since.

"'The challenge,' he said, 'is to realize that something is fulfilling because we individually determine it is fulfilling, not because someone else tells us it is.'

"That night when I got home, I sat and reflected on what was fulfilling for me and why. I challenged myself to think about how I wanted to spend each day. Before long, I was asking myself why I wanted to spend each day that way. Eventually, that line of thinking led me to here," she said.

I looked down. Anne was pointing at the menu.

*Why are you here?*

"And then?" I asked.

Anne laughed again. "Well, I think Casey probably already explained to you that once you ask yourself *Why am I here?*, things change for you. Without going into all the drawn-out details, I can tell you that ever since that night, I haven't been the same.

"It started slowly, with me taking a little more time for myself each week. I stopped treating myself to 'things' as compensation for working so hard, and instead started treating myself by doing what I wanted to do. Each day I made sure I spent at least one hour doing something I really liked. Sometimes it was reading a novel I was excited about. Other days it was going for a long walk or playing sports.

"Eventually, the one hour became two, and that progressed to three. Before I knew it, I was totally focused on doing things I wanted to do, things that fulfilled my answer to 'why am I here?'"

## ꩜ **Thirteen**

A nne turned to Mike. "Have you had the death discussion yet?"

"The what?" I asked, suddenly feeling more than a little apprehensive.

Anne smiled, and pointed to the menu. "The second question."

I looked down.

*Do you fear death?*

I'd almost forgotten about the other two questions on the menu. After all I'd been exposed to with the first one, I wasn't sure I was ready to think about the others.

"They're related," said Mike.

There was that mind reading thing again. Just when I was starting to think this place was a normal café.

Actually, I guess I never thought that. "What do you mean by 'related'?" I asked.

"Do you fear death?" asked Anne. "Most people do. As a matter of fact it's one of the most common fears people have."

"I don't know," I replied. "There's a lot to do in life, and I don't want to die before I have a chance to experience all the things I want. But death isn't something I think about every day."

"People who haven't asked themselves the question you saw on the menu, and haven't taken the steps to fulfill their PFE with what they want to do," . . . Anne looked at me and paused . . . "those people fear death."

It was my turn to pause. I looked at Anne and Mike. "Are you saying most people spend every day thinking about death? I'm not sure I believe that. I mean I certainly don't spend every day thinking about it."

Mike smiled. "No, it's not like that. What we're describing takes place primarily on the unconscious level. Most people don't have the concept of death at the forefront of their thinking every day. But unconsciously, they know that as each day passes, they are another day closer to not having a chance to do what they want in life. So they fear the day that exists sometime in the future when they will no longer *have* the chance. They fear the day they will die."

I thought about what he'd just said. "But it doesn't have to be like that, does it? I mean if someone asked themselves why they are here, chose the things they want to do that would fulfill their PFE, and then actually did them, then why would they fear death? You can't fear not having the chance to do something if you've already done it, or you're doing it every day."

Anne smiled. "No you can't," she said softly. She got up from the table. "It's been a pleasure meeting you, John. I'm afraid I need to get back to my friend, but I've enjoyed our conversation."

I stood up and we shook hands. "I have as well," I said. "Thanks for sharing your insights with me."

As she turned and walked to her table, I slid back into the booth. I felt different. I wasn't sure how, but I felt like I'd just learned something that was going to be very valuable for a long time.

Mike got up from the table. "Are you all right, John? You look a little stunned."

"Just thinking," I replied. "What you and Anne were talking about makes a lot of sense. I'm surprised I haven't heard it before or thought of it myself."

"Everything in its own time, John. You *may* have thought of it before, but at that time you weren't ready to listen to or act on those thoughts."

Mike reached down and took two of the empty plates from the table. "Why don't I clear away some of these dishes for you. Are you still working on the hash browns?"

"Amazingly, yes," I said, drawing myself out of my thoughts and back to the food in front of me. "They're too good, and I'm still too hungry to let them go."

As Mike walked away from the table, I refocused on all the things he, Anne, and I had just discussed. It was a lot to digest. I thought about Anne's story and the impact of advertisements. How much of my definition of success, happiness, and fulfillment *had been* determined by people other than myself? It was hard to know. I decided that going forward I would try to be more aware of the messages behind what people were saying.

The discussion about death was something entirely different. I knew I'd come to a deeper level of understanding at the end of our conversation. It wasn't that I'd been living in a state of emotional despair, just worrying about death. It wasn't even something I thought about often. But the concept of living a life that fulfills my own purpose, and the impact that would have on how I viewed each day, resonated very well with me.

"You can't fear not having the chance to do something if you've already done it, or you're doing it every day," I said to myself.

I wished I *had* thought of or heard that sooner. "Still," I reflected, "it's not enough to know the concept. The point is to actually do the things I want to do."

## Fourteen

I looked down at the menu again.
*Why are you here?*
*Do you fear death?*
*Are you fulfilled?*

The questions didn't seem as odd compared to when I first read them off the menu. In fact, they were much more important now.

*Are you fulfilled?*

"Until you go beyond merely knowing why you are here, and actually start working towards it, I don't think you can be fulfilled," I thought to myself.

"But doing that isn't always so easy, is it?" asked Casey.

I looked up as she reached for my water glass. "No, no it's not," I said. "I'm thinking of my own situation. I know how to do what I do every day. I get paid for it.

What happens if I ask myself why I'm here, and identify what I want to do, and then I don't know how to do those things? Or what if I can't get a job doing them? What will I do for money?

"How can I support myself, and how can I save for retirement? What if I'm not good at whatever these new things might be? Or what if they're things other people will laugh at or not respect?"

Casey waited until I'd finished. "John, do you think once a person goes through the steps to identify why they are here and comes up with the true answer, that they'll be excited about what they've discovered?"

I paused for a second, trying to envision what that would be like. "I hope so," I replied. "If they've truly figured out why they exist, I would think that's very exciting."

"Do you think it would be equally exciting to do things that help fulfill the reason?" she asked.

I paused again. The questions seemed too easy. "I must be missing something," I thought. "Sure," I said. "Why wouldn't it be? A person should be more excited and passionate about that than anything else."

"Then why do you think the person might fail?"

I looked at her. Before I could respond, she continued.

"Have you ever met someone who was completely passionate about what they did every day? They seemed to be spending their time on something they truly enjoyed?"

I paused again. "Not many. But I know a few people who fit that description."

"Are they good at what they do?" Casey asked.

"Well, yeah," I replied a little sarcastically. "With all the time they spend on it, they should be good at it. I mean they read about it in their free time, they watch TV shows about it, they go to conventions on it. . . . With all that exposure, they should be good at what they do."

"Don't they get tired of doing what they do?" she asked.

"No," I replied. "They can't seem to get enough of it. It's like they get charged by doing it, and. . . ." I stopped in mid-sentence.

Casey smiled at me. "Do they seem to have much trouble finding work?"

I paused again. "Not the people who I know. They have so much knowledge about what they like to do, and are so passionate about it, that everyone always goes to them for advice and wants them involved in what they're doing."

"I would imagine they're pretty positive and upbeat people," she said. "They probably don't need to get away from it all to get 'recharged.'"

I let Casey's comments sink in. It was an interesting way to look at things. What would life be like if I was always doing the things I wanted to do? What if I was always spending my time on something I was passionate about? "But how about the money?" I asked. "Just because you're good at something, or know a lot about it, doesn't mean you can get paid a lot for it. You might always be able to find work, but will it pay well?" I felt a little better about myself for having come up with that one. "After all," I continued, "who knows what kinds of things a person would consider fulfilling."

"I see," said Casey. "Well, let's think of a worst possible scenario regarding the money. A person could live a life where every day they do what they have identified as something that will fulfill their Purpose For Existing. However, they don't make 'a lot' of money. My, that would be tragic.

"Imagine the consequences. You could find yourself having lived your life in a way that always fulfilled your PFE. You could spend your entire life doing what you want to do, because you figured out why you are here. But . . . you might reach the age of sixty-five and not have sufficient retirement savings.

"What to do then?" she asked, her voice filled with mock drama. "I guess you would just have to keep on doing the things you want to do. That could indeed be tragic."

I laughed. "Casey, you can be downright sarcastic when you want to be."

She smiled back at me. "I'm just trying to make sure I completely understand your line of thinking."

"I get it, I get it. It goes back to Mike's story about the fisherman. Why wait to do what you want, when you can do it right now."

"It's that, and something more. Do you remember your conversation with Anne about why some people buy things?"

"Sure, we were talking about how some people seek more money so they can buy more things. They hope what they purchase will fulfill them, since they aren't doing what they want to be doing every day. But the danger is, the more they buy, the more they have to work to pay for what they bought. If they aren't careful, it becomes a downward spiral."

I paused. It felt like there was a piece I was missing. I looked at Casey, but she just looked straight back at me. "It has to do with the worst possible scenario, doesn't it?" I asked. Casey nodded.

I thought for a moment. "I guess the first thing is that a person in the worst-case scenario could always choose to do something else."

Casey just nodded again, so I continued.

"And, that is the worst possible scenario. Obviously there is a better scenario. A person could get paid a lot of money for doing the things they want to do and that fulfill why they are here."

Casey nodded once more.

I knew I still hadn't gotten to what it was I felt was missing. I sat back against the bench and took a drink of water. I was just about to ask for a hint, when it struck me. "Maybe the money becomes less relevant. I mean it would depend on the person and the circumstances, but thinking back to the conversation I had with Anne, I remember wondering why people work to begin with. When Anne and I were talking, we discussed that part of the reason for working tied back to seeking fulfillment."

"Can you give me an example?" asked Casey.

"Well, the reason I work is to make money," I replied. "I need money to pay for the things I buy. When I think about all the things I buy, I believe I'm a little bit like the people Anne and I were talking about. A lot of what I own are things that help me escape for a while, things that help me unwind and make me feel better about my surroundings.

"What I'm wondering, is how much of that would I want if I didn't have the need to 'escape,' or 'unwind'? If I was always doing what I wanted to be doing, then there should be less to escape from, and probably not nearly as much stress to be unwound from, either. I'm not saying I would go live in a shack in the woods somewhere, but I'm wondering if a person's definition of 'a lot of money' varies based on how much they're living a life that fulfills their PFE."

Casey nodded again. "So are you suggesting that people should stop wanting to have more money?"

"No," I said, and tried to find the right words to explain what I was thinking.

"That's not what I mean. I'm just saying that for myself, I think if I figured out why I am here, and I was doing the things I determined would fulfill that—then I'd probably be less concerned about money than I am. That's all I'm trying to say."

Casey got up from the table and picked up two of my empty plates. She smiled, "Interesting thoughts, John."

I watched her walk back toward the kitchen.

"This is an interesting place."

## ↷ Fifteen

When Casey returned, she refilled my water glass and sat down across from me. "John, when I took your dishes to the kitchen, Mike reminded me about something you might find interesting. It relates to the discussion we were having on the challenges people might face when they're trying to fulfill their PFE."

"You mean like my question about how do they make money?"

"That's part of it, and there's more."

I looked at Casey. "I'd like to hear about it."

"For this to work," she began, "I need you to think of some of those people who we were talking about earlier."

"You mean the ones I know who are completely passionate about what they're doing?" I asked. "The ones who seem to spend each day doing what they truly enjoy?"

"Those are the ones. Did you notice anything about them?"

"Well, one woman was doing sales in a . . . "

"Actually, John," Casey interjected, "think more broadly than what they were doing. What did you notice overall about them?"

I sat back and closed my eyes for a moment. I could picture in my mind the people I was thinking of. "Well, as I mentioned before, they all seem genuinely happy. They appear to enjoy what they're doing. They're also really confident. It doesn't come across as false bravado either. They just seem to know things will go the way they want them to.

"This might sound strange, but another characteristic is that they're all lucky. I mean, good things just happen for them, unexpected things."

"Can you give me an example?" Casey asked.

"Well, there's this one woman I'm thinking of. She's in advertising, which seems a little strange after my earlier conversation with Anne. Anyway, she was trying to land a big account. I don't even know what it was for anymore, but I remember it was a big deal and a lot of other people had tried for it and failed.

"Well, she decided she wanted to land it. Two weeks into working on the materials for her presentation, she received a call from an old college friend. She hadn't spoken with this person in a long time. While they were catching up, they got on the topic of work, and the woman mentioned how she was trying to get this account. It turned out that the college friend had another friend who worked at the very company the woman was going after.

"A few phone calls later, the three of them met for dinner. Sure enough, a few weeks after that, the woman got the account. That's what I mean by unexpected things happening for them. Those people just seem to be very lucky."

"Why do you think that is, John?" asked Casey.

I drank some of my water. "I don't know exactly. Maybe it's just coincidence. The funny thing is though, you asked me to think about the people who truly enjoy what they're doing. They're the ones spending time on things that seem to be in line with their PFE. These types of lucky events seems to happen all the time for those people."

Casey smiled and looked at me. "Does it only happen for those people? Has that type of thing ever happened to you?"

I sat back against the seat of the booth. "I suppose it has. I mean, I can't think of a particular instance off the top of my head, but I know there have been times when I was amazed at how something unexpected happened just when I needed it to."

"John, if you were able to remember those specific instances, I have a hunch you would find a common link between them."

"Such as maybe those were times when I was doing exactly what I wanted to be doing?" I asked. As I said it, I felt a shudder run through me. It was the same feeling I had earlier, when it seemed like I learned something significant about myself.

"I can't speak for you specifically, John, but in working here at the café, I've noticed some things about people in general. The ones who know their PFE, and are doing whatever they want to fulfill it, do seem very lucky. Unexpected, seemingly random things happen for them just when they need it most.

"I've asked some of them about it, and while they all agree it exists, not too many have the same opinion about what might cause it. To be honest, most of them aren't really concerned with identifying exactly what it is. They know it comes into play when they are fulfilling their Purpose For Existing, and they just see it as part of the way things work."

"Strange," I replied. "It sounds a little mystical."

"Some people have said that. Others see it as part of the natural flow of the universe, or a higher power at work. Still others just view it as good luck. But they all agree it's there and is a factor in what they do."

"What do you think, Casey?"

This time it was she who had to pause for a moment. "Honestly, I don't know. I suppose it's all those reasons and maybe one other. Have you ever heard of the theory of exponential numbers?"

"I'm not sure. Can you explain it to me?"

"Sure, it's really pretty easy. I'll give you an example. The theory of exponential numbers is that if you tell someone something, and you can get them to tell other people, and those other people tell still more people, then before long, your message has reached many more people than you personally talked to."

"Kind of like passing along an e-mail," I said, "where you send it to ten people, and then they send it to ten more people, and it keeps on going."

"Exactly. It's the same concept. Only now, suppose you're letting people know about something you're trying to do that will help fulfill your PFE. If you share it with ten people, and they each share it with ten and it keeps going, before long you have a whole bunch of people who potentially will help you."

I thought for a moment. "But why would they be willing to help me? What would motivate people to talk with others about what I'm trying to do?"

Casey looked at me but didn't respond. I got the impression this was another one of those times when I was supposed to answer my own question. I thought about our current conversation and how we'd gotten to the topic of exponential numbers. The solution wasn't coming to me, though. "I'm not sure I get it Casey. How about a hint?"

"John, remember those people you thought of when we started this conversation—the ones who are working to fulfill their PFEs? How does it feel when you interact with them?"

"It feels great. You can't help but get caught up in their passion and enthusiasm for what they're doing. You just feel like you want to help them."

I paused again. "Oh come on, Casey. Are you telling me that's the answer? But how does that apply to the message being passed along?"

"John, you just said their passion and enthusiasm makes you feel like you want to help. If you couldn't help, but you knew others who might be able to, would you contact them?"

"Sure. You feel inspired to because they seem so . . . " I paused, looking for the right words.

"On the right path?" asked Casey.

"Yeah, something like that. They seem so on the right path that you just want to help."

"And when you talk about them to other people who might be able to help, how do you speak of them?" Casey asked.

I smiled, half to myself, and half to Casey. "I speak with some of the same passion and enthusiasm as they originally spoke to me. It's catching, and almost as if the emotion stays with the story, or with the need."

"Perhaps that's your answer." Casey stood and gathered the remaining dishes from the table. "I'm impressed, John," she commented, holding the empty plates. "You must have been really hungry."

"It's the food," I replied. "It's too good to pass up."

I glanced at the kitchen and saw Mike. He waved, and I waved back, feeling a little less self-conscious this time about the whole waving to cooks in a diner concept. "Casey, I don't suppose there's still a piece of that strawberry-rhubarb pie left?"

She laughed. "I'll head back to the kitchen and see what I can do."

## ⌒ Sixteen

A few minutes later, Mike arrived at the table. On the plate in his hand was a piece of pie large enough for four people. "One piece of strawberry-rhubarb pie?" he asked.

"Mike, that looks like half the pie. I'm not sure I can handle all that."

He set an extra napkin and a new fork down on the table, along with the plate. "Take your time, no hurry. How was your discussion with Casey?"

By this time I'd already taken a large forkful of pie and was in the process of chewing it. I chased it down with some water and swallowed, "It was interesting, very interesting. We were talking about people who seem to have answered the modified version of this question," I said, and pointed to the menu.

For a moment, the words on the menu transformed to *"Why am I here?"* and then slowly returned to *"Why are you here?"* I didn't even bother mentioning the change.

"Right, that one," I continued. "Those people seem to have some common characteristics in that they know why they are here, they've figured out what things they want to do to fulfill that reason, and they're completely confident they'll be able to do those things. And when they try to do them, events occur to help them succeed. Casey was explaining to me some of the theories people have on that last part."

Mike grinned. "There's a lot of speculation about that one. There has been for a long time, possibly back to the oldest philosophers."

"Mike, I'm a little confused about something. Why doesn't everyone go after their PFE? What is it that holds them back? And before you start, I know I should ask that question of myself, and I was doing so when you walked up. But I'm curious to know if there's a bigger, more encompassing reason than any I might have just for myself."

Mike took a sip from the mug he was holding and set it on the table as he sat down across from me. "Certainly each of us has our own reasons," he began. "And those reasons are something every person has to address themselves, since they are unique to their own situation. There are some bigger items that seem to dominate, though."

"For example?"

"Well, for many people it's as simple as never having been exposed to the concept of a Purpose For Existing. Others understand the concept, but they aren't sure they have a PFE. Then there are some people who because of their upbringing, environment, or perhaps religious beliefs, don't believe they have the right to try and fulfill their PFE.

"Even people who feel they have a Purpose For Existing, and believe they have the right to fulfill it, sometimes don't believe fulfilling it is as simple as knowing they can, and then doing what they want.

"This goes back to some of what you and Anne were talking about. Many people make their living or get their power by convincing others that they, or something they make or sell, are the key to fulfillment. Imagine the challenge for them if people came to the realization that we each control our own level of fulfillment. The people trying to convince others would lose their power. For those types of people, losing power over others is not something that sounds appealing."

"That reminds me of one of the conversations Casey and I had earlier tonight," I said. "She helped me understand that once someone knows their PFE, they get to do and become whatever they want. They don't need someone else's permission or consent."

"Correct. And on top of that, no one can keep a person from, or enable them to, achieve and do all they want in life. We each control our own destiny."

I thought about that, and on my earlier conversations with Casey and Anne. "What you're describing is very different from the messages I see and hear in my every-day life. I understand why it's so hard for people to even be exposed to the concepts of identifying why they exist and of controlling their own destiny—let alone taking the next steps and actually living that way."

"Absolutely," said Mike. "But it's not impossible. As a matter of fact, a couple of weeks ago a visitor to the café told Casey and me an interesting story about how he learned about controlling his own destiny. If you're interested, I'll share it with you."

"Definitely. Does it involve more fishermen?"

Mike laughed, "Not this time, but it does involve sports. For years this guy had a recurring dream where he was standing over a very tough golf shot. As he explained it, he isn't a very good golfer when he's awake, so to face this challenge while sleeping was particularly frustrating. In his dream, the ball he needed to hit was sitting on a window ledge, or on a large down-sloping rock, or someplace equally ridiculous and challenging.

"He would try and try to plant his feet and get a good practice swing, but it never felt right and he knew the shot would be poor. The more practice swings he took, the more anxious and stressed he became.

"As his frustration peaked, he would finally feel like he was ready to take the shot. However, as he started his back swing, the location of the ball would change, and he would be faced with a new, equally challenging lie. He would then go through another buildup of stress and anxiety. This cycle kept repeating until he would finally wake up with his heart pounding and his body full of stress.

"One night he had the same dream, but at the point where he typically reached his maximum level of frustration, he was suddenly aware he could just pick up the ball and put it somewhere else. Nothing was at stake, and no one but he cared where he hit the ball from.

"He said he woke up with an incredibly strong sense of having gained a major insight into something that once he knew it seemed so obvious, but hadn't before. We ended our conversation with him explaining to me that 'Despite what we may be taught to believe, or what we hear in advertising, or feel when we are stressed out at work, we each control every moment of our lives. I had forgotten that, and was trying to adjust to all kinds of other influences, as I was letting them control my life.

"'Just like no one really cared about where I hit the golf ball from except me, in life only you truly know what you want from your existence. Don't ever let things or people drive you to the point where you feel you no longer have control over your own destiny. Be active in choosing your path, or it will be chosen for you. Just move the golf ball.'"

Mike finished the story and looked at me. "See, no fishermen."

"No fishermen indeed, but a great story nonetheless. I like the message in there."

"So did the guy. He said the message in the dream changed his life. From that point on, he realized he was in charge of choosing his own destiny. Now, whenever he encounters something and isn't sure what to do, he just tells himself to move the golf ball. He said merely speaking the words reminds him to not be afraid, and just do whatever he wants."

## ๑๙ **Seventeen**

I looked at my watch. It was 5:15 in the morning. "I can't believe it," I said. "It's almost time for me to order breakfast again."

Mike smiled, "First you might want to finish off your pie."

"With pleasure," I replied, and grabbed another forkful. I finished chewing and took another sip of water. "Mike, there's something I'm still unsure of. I've talked about it with both you and Casey, but I don't have the answer yet."

Mike smiled, "Ask away. Unless it's for the pie recipe. That's one of the few pieces of information we keep secret here. It was my mom's and I promised her I'd never give it away."

I grinned, "I understand. Luckily, I'm looking for a different answer. We've talked about people asking themselves, 'Why am I here?' and Casey and I discussed both the ramifications of asking that question, and also what people can do once they know the answer. What I still don't know is . . . "

"How you go about finding the answer," said Mike.

"Right."

"I think for that one I better call Casey over. Perhaps she and I combined can give you a better answer than just one of us." Mike got up from the table and walked to the far end of the restaurant, where Casey was sitting and talking with Anne and her friend. I wondered if they were discussing some of the same things I was.

A moment later, Casey got up and she and Mike walked back to me.

"How's the pie?" Casey asked as the two of them sat down.

"Excellent," I said with a grin. "I'm almost full."

"Casey, John was asking about how someone finds the answer to the first question," Mike said. He pointed to the *"Why are you here?"* on the back of the menu, which transformed into *"Why am I here?"* "I thought perhaps both of us could try and answer his questions."

Casey nodded, then looked directly into my eyes. In a very serious voice she asked, "Do you have a mailbox, John?"

"Sure."

"Well, on the first full moon that falls on the seventh day of the month after you have asked the question, a package will arrive in your mailbox. In that package is a document, which if held over a candle will display a hidden message from those who know the answer. The message can only be read once in your life, and only by candlelight, and has to be read on the seventh."

I stopped drinking and leaned forward to hear the rest of what she was saying.

"When you open the package, you will know it is the correct one, because the ribbon will be red, and tied in a double knot, with the . . . "

At this point, I noticed the table was moving—in fact, it seemed to be vibrating. I sat back in my seat.

"What's going on, Casey?" I asked, surprised. "The table. . . ."

Casey continued on, as if she didn't notice the table was shaking. ". . . with the larger loop at least two times bigger than the smaller loop, and located in the upper left-hand corner of the package."

I glanced at Mike. To my surprise and slight embarrassment, I realized the table shaking was not a sign from the netherworld, as I had begun to think it might be. Instead, it was caused by Mike. He had been listening to Casey, and to contain his laughter, had put his hand over his mouth and leaned on the table. He was laughing so hard his whole body was shaking, and in turn it was causing the table to shake.

I started to laugh. Casey turned to Mike and gave him a playful punch in the shoulder.

"You're not a very good accomplice," she said with a smile.

"I'm sorry," said Mike. "You were just too convincing. I couldn't contain myself."

"Okay," said Casey, "so I might have been taking a little bit of creative liberty regarding the answer to your question, John."

"A little bit!" said Mike. "I'd say that was downright fabrication. Tied in a double knot, with . . . " Mike finished his imitation of Casey, and we all started to laugh again.

"You're quite a storyteller, Casey," I said. "However, I'm afraid you still haven't answered my question."

"In addition to having a little fun," she said with a smile, "I was trying to make a point. For some people, they ask the question, and they want to know the answer, but they want someone or something else to be responsible for bringing them the answer."

"In a package that arrives on the seventh," I said, and smiled.

"Right, on the seventh. The thing is, just as we have free will to decide what we want to do once we know the answer, we are also the ones in control of finding the answer."

"So what you're saying," I began, "is you can't just take the first step and then wait around. If someone really wants to know why they are here, they have to figure out the answer for themselves."

"Exactly," said Mike. "And people do that in different ways. Some spend time meditating on why they are here. Others listen to their favorite music and note where their mind takes them. Many people take time alone in a natural environment, and still others talk with friends and strangers about it. Some people are guided to their answer through ideas and stories they read in books."

"Do you have a recommendation for which one works best?" I asked.

Casey turned to me. "It really depends on the person, John. The key thing to remember is, we are the only ones who can determine what *our* answer is. That's one reason why many people spend some time by themselves while they are seeking it."

"I can understand that," I said. "It's hard to focus on something when you're being bombarded by information and messages from all around you."

"Right," Mike replied. "When people take time to meditate or be alone in a natural environment, they're usually trying to get away from the external 'noise,' so they can focus on what *they* really think."

"Is that all there is to it?" I asked.

"Not completely," Casey replied. "John, do you remember when we were talking about the value in getting exposure to other ideas, cultures, perspectives, people, and things like that?"

"Sure, when we were discussing how a person could find out about the different things they could do to fulfill their Purpose For Existing."

"Exactly," Casey replied. "The same idea applies to people trying to figure out what their PFE is. Some find that when they experience new things and learn new ideas, certain ones resonate with them. Many people actually experience a physical reaction. They get chills, a tremor up their spine, or cry tears of joy when they come across something they really relate to. For others, a sense of knowing comes over them. Those can be clues to help people identify their answer to why they are here."

"I know what you're talking about," I said and smiled. "I've had that happen before, when I read or heard something and I just knew it was right for me. As a matter of fact, I've had a number of those moments tonight."

Casey smiled back. "Did we answer your question, John?"

"I think so. If I understand you correctly, there's no single answer for everyone, but putting yourself in a position where you can focus on the question is one possible way. Getting exposure to different experiences and ideas, and watching for personal reactions to them, is something else that can help."

"You got it," said Mike.

Casey got up from the table. "I'm going to check on our other guests. Is there anything else you need, John?"

"I don't think so, Casey, thanks. Unless I receive an unexpected package with red ribbon, delivered after a full moon . . . . Then I'll probably have a few more questions."

She laughed and winked at Mike, "Fair enough. You let us know."

## ᏜᏜ **Eighteen**

"John, where were you heading when you stopped in here?" Mike asked, as Casey walked away from the table.

"I'm starting my vacation. I felt like I needed some time away from everything—an opportunity to think. Even though I didn't specifically know what I wanted to think about. I have to say, in the last . . . " I glanced at my watch, ". . . the last eight hours, I've gotten some pretty good ideas for that.

"Mike, do you mind if I ask you a personal question?"

"Not at all, what is it?"

I looked at him. "What made *you* ask the question on the menu?"

Mike sat back and a smile crept onto his face. "What makes you so sure I have?"

"You, your demeanor, this place. I don't know for sure, but I get the feeling you're doing exactly what you want to be doing. I assume you asked the question at some point, and this place is the result."

Mike smiled again and took a sip from his mug. "A number of years ago I was living a pretty hectic life. I was going to graduate school at night, working full time during the day, and filling every other minute training for and trying to make it as a professional athlete. For two-and-a-half years, almost every moment of my life was scheduled.

"When I graduated, I quit my job and took the summer off, since I'd already lined up a new job that would start at the beginning of September. A buddy of mine and I decided to go down to Costa Rica to celebrate our respective graduations. He had just completed school also.

"We spent weeks traveling around the country, hiking through rain forests, seeing wildlife, and getting immersed in a new culture. Then one day we were sitting on a log, eating fresh mangos and watching the waves crash against this unbelievably beautiful beach. We'd spent the afternoon bodysurfing in the eighty-five-degree water and were relaxing and watching the sky turn from brilliant blue to pink, orange, and red as the sun began to set."

"That sounds pretty spectacular," I said.

"It was. And I remember looking out at the entire scene and coming to the realization that while I had been planning every minute of my life for the last two-and-a-half years, this scene had been repeating itself every day. Paradise had been just a few hours' plane flight and some dirt roads away, and I didn't even know it existed. And I realized, not only had it existed for the two-and-a-half years I was so busy, but the sun had been setting there, and the waves had been crashing upon that beach, for millions if not billions of years.

"As that realization came over me, I felt very small. My problems, the things I had stressed about, my worries about the future, all seemed completely unimportant. I knew no matter what I did or didn't do during my life, whether my decisions were right, wrong, or somewhere in the middle, all of this would still be going on long after I was no longer alive.

"I sat there, faced with the unbelievable beauty and grandeur of nature and the realization that my life was an infinitesimal piece of something much bigger. Then I was struck by the thought, *so why am I here? If all the things I thought were so important really aren't, then what is? What is my purpose for existing? Why am I here?*

"Once I had those questions in my head, I went through something similar to what Casey described to you. They were always with me until I figured out the answers."

I sat back in my seat. I hadn't realized it, but as Mike was speaking I was leaning forward to catch every part of what he was saying.

"Thanks, Mike. That's an amazing story."

"Life is an amazing story, John. It's just that some people don't realize they are the author, and they can write it however they want."

Mike got up from the table. "I'm going to head back and start cleaning up the kitchen a bit. Is there anything else you need, John?"

"No, I think I'm going to hit the road pretty soon. Speaking of which, I was pretty lost when I found this place. I don't really know which direction I'm supposed to go now."

Mike smiled. "Well, that depends on where you want to get to."

He started to say something else, and then paused as if he decided against it. When he spoke again, it was obviously on a different thought. "If you continue on for a few miles down this road, you'll come to a four-way intersection. Take a right, and that will get you back to the highway. There's a gas station just before the entrance ramp. You have enough gas to make it there."

I didn't know how he knew I had enough gas to make it to the station, but I had a hunch he would end up being right. I stood up from the table and extended my hand. "Thanks, Mike. You've got a very special place here."

He took my hand and shook it. "You're welcome, John. Good luck with your journey." With that, he turned and walked away.

## ୭୦ **Nineteen**

I looked down at the menu.
*Why are you here?*
*Do you fear death?*
*Are you fulfilled?*

They were deep questions. If someone had asked me them a day earlier, I'd have thought that person was a little out of it. Now, as I sat reading the back of the menu, I couldn't imagine not having been exposed to them.

Casey came by the table, put down my check, and handed me a container. "It's the last piece of straw-berry-rhubarb pie. A parting gift from Mike.

"And this is from me," she said, and handed me a menu. On the front, underneath the words "The Why

Are You Here Café," Casey had written a message to me. I read it, and then read it again.

"A little something to remember us by," she said and smiled.

"Thank you, Casey. Thank you for everything."

"My pleasure, John. That's what we are here for."

I left some money on the table, picked up the menu and the container of pie, and walked out of the café into the beginning of a new day.

The sun had just started to rise above the trees in the field across from the gravel parking lot. The air held both the last remnants of stillness that precede the start of a new day, and at the same time, the sounds of a day already in motion.

I felt refreshed and alive. I shifted the container I was carrying from my right hand to my left, and opened the door to my car.

"Why am I here?" I thought to myself, "Why am I here . . . ?"

It was indeed, a very new day.

## ∽ **Epilogue**

After my night in the café, things changed for me. They weren't lightning-bolt-from-the-sky-type changes in terms of how they presented themselves, but they were at least that dynamic in their eventual impact on my life.

Like Anne, I started slowly. I left the café wondering, "Why am I here?" and continued to ponder that question for the rest of my time off. The answers did not all come right away. I learned that finding my Purpose For Existing, or PFE, as Casey called it, required more than just spending a vacation thinking about it, and then returning to everything I had been doing. Like most things worth knowing, it took some effort to uncover the answer.

It was a combination of methods I learned from Casey and Anne that eventually enabled me to figure it out. I started with a small amount of time each day that I dedicated to doing things I liked, which was similar to the technique Anne had used. Then I tried to take advantage of the opportunities Casey talked about and sought chances to learn and try new things. This helped me expand my universe of possible reasons for why I am here, so it was not as small as it had been when I started my journey.

Eventually, my PFE, and the ways I want to fulfill it, became clear. Ironically, that was when I faced the most difficult challenge of all. When you weigh two choices, and one is living a life that fulfills your Purpose For Existing, and the other is just living, you would think the decision is simple.

It isn't.

Over time, I have observed that this is the place where most people end their journey. They peer through a hole in the fence, and can clearly see the life they would like to have, but for any number of reasons, they don't open the gate and walk into that life.

Initially, this caused me a great deal of sorrow. But as Mike said, and I have come to believe, people make that choice at all different times in their lives. Some make it when they are children, some later, and some never do. It can't be rushed, and it can't be anyone's decision but theirs.

For me, the knowledge that "you can't fear not having the chance to do something if you are doing it or have already done it" helped me push open that gate. It is now one of the philosophies by which I live my life.

Not a day goes by when I don't think of something associated with the café. I'm reminded of Casey and her story of the green sea turtle every time I open my mailbox and see it filled with advertisements and offers for things I don't need. That incoming wave is always present, ready to sap my time and energy. But now I know it exists, and I save my strength for the outgoing waves.

I also often think of Mike's story of sitting on the beach in Costa Rica. Viewed from a big picture perspective, our stresses, anxieties, victories, and losses account for little.

Yet it is in the face of our seeming insignificance that we find meaning.

If I have any regret about making the changes I've made in my life, it is only that I didn't make them sooner. I guess I just wasn't ready before that night in the café.

Now, having sought out why I am here, and living my life to fulfill that reason, I would never go back to a life on the other side of the gate.

Thank you for reading *The Why Café*.

We invite you to stay connected with John and share in a like spirited community:

 http://www.facebook.com/bigfiveforlife

 @johnpstrelecky

Receive a free copy of John's article "Ten Tips for Living the Life of Your Dreams," by joining this Fan Page:

 http://www.facebook.com/bigfiveforlife

To have John speak at your upcoming event, visit;
www.johnpstrelecky.com

To preview *Life Safari*, John's follow-up book to *The Why Café,* simply turn the page.

# LIFE
# SAFARI

*John P. Strelecky*

**Aspen Light Publishing**

From the author of the international bestseller *The Why Café*, comes this much anticipated next work—an inspiring and emotionally powerful story set amidst the mystery, beauty, and allure of Africa.

Jack is a young man struggling to find happiness in his life. Although he doesn't know why, the one image that seems to capture his soul is that of Africa. With solitary focus, he saves for two years and then embarks on a journey to find the source of the calling he has felt.

Halfway around the world, a very old, very wise African woman named Ma Ma Gombe is on a journey of her own. She is seeking a fabled destination she was told of as a child—"a place where you can see the earth be born, and then watch the world go to sleep, a place so beautiful that words cannot describe it." It is a destination known to her only as "the birthplace of all."

As if their paths were destined to intertwine, these two unlikely travelers meet shortly after Jack's arrival in Africa and join together on a journey that changes both of their lives forever.

Walk with them as they cross the African continent on foot. Marvel with them at the animals they encounter, the people they meet, and the adventures they experience. Like Jack, find through the teachings of Ma Ma Gombe that piece of your soul yearning to be set free.

In *Life Safari*, John P. Strelecky has created a story that inspires and taps the spirit for adventure in readers everywhere. A tale that will touch your emotions, open your eyes to the amazing continent of Africa, and open your heart to the amazing potential within all of us.

*"There is a place inside our soul where we hold our greatest wishes. Those wishes are our Big Five for Life."*

—Ma Ma Gombe

# 1

I picked up the leather-bound notebook that had been my constant companion throughout the journey. The pages were weather-beaten and torn from the effects of rain and sun and the sheer challenges that came with crossing a continent on foot.

Much had transpired since then, but each time I held that journal I was instantly transported back. And each time, the memory began the same way, with my entrance into Africa.

How long ago that seemed, and yet how powerful was the experience—powerful enough that it has remained a permanent part of my soul. After all, I almost died there. After all, I found my life there.

I didn't know what to expect when I began my journey to Africa. Other than pictures I had seen in books, I knew almost nothing about the people, the

animals, or the environment I would encounter. But at the time, none of that seemed to matter. I knew one thing, and that one thing was enough. I knew I needed to be happy. For some reason, I thought Africa was the place where I would find my happiness.

I opened the journal. There it was: Day 1. I had noted it as such with a single statement. "Today, the adventure begins." And indeed it had. I crossed to Africa by ship. The journey took the better part of three weeks. When I left home, I carried nothing more than a large backpack full of clothes, basic camping supplies, good hiking boots, an oversized hat to protect myself from the sun, and the money I'd saved over the course of two years.

Two years was the time it took me to go from the start of my dream to the beginning of my reality. Two years may seem like a long time to wait to pursue one's dream, but not when compared to the lifetime most people spend. Many a person during those two years had expressed how they also would love to go to Africa. Initially I tried to explain that if I could do it so could they. I certainly wasn't the highest paid person among them. As a matter of fact, I was probably one of the lowest.

But I soon realized that they weren't truly serious about going to Africa, or else they would be going. They liked to talk about their dreams, but in the end, they just left them as dreams. They didn't know what I had felt a glimpse of, and what Ma Ma Gombe would confirm for me. That dreams are in fact realities waiting to happen. But they don't wait forever. At some point you have to help them make the transition. Or eventually, they just fade away.

So there I stood, a six-foot-one-inch, twenty-two-year-old kid. Having been an athlete most of my life, I was relatively lean but muscular. To a stranger I would have seemed quietly confident without being cocky— a little unsure of my future and yet hopeful that I was heading in the right direction.

My ancestors had come from Eastern Europe, and I'd inherited the genes of a mix of nations. My blonde hair and blue eyes were like my mother's, my ability to tan quickly to a deep brown hue reflected more of my father's family.

And there I was—in Africa.

# To continue
# this Africa
# adventure,
# visit

## www.thelifesafari.com

## ♋ About the Author

Following a life changing event when he was thirty-three years old, John was inspired to sit down and tell the story of *The Why Café*. He had no previous experience or academic training as a writer.

Within a year after its release, word of mouth support from readers had spread the book across the globe—inspiring people on every continent, including Antarctica. It went on to become a #1 Best Seller, and translated into twenty-one languages. John has since written other books, including *Life Safari* and *The Big Five for Life*. He coauthored the book *How to be Rich and Happy*.

Through his writings and appearances on television and radio, John's messages have inspired millions of people to live life on their terms. He has been honored alongside Oprah Winfrey, Wayne Dyer, and Deepak Chopra as one of the one hundred most inspirational thought leaders in the field of leadership and personal development. All of this continues to humble and amaze him.

To learn more about John, or to inquire about his availability for interviews and as a speaker, please visit;

www.bigfiveforlife.com

## ⤺ Reader's Guide

**The Why Café** by John P. Strelecky

FOR DISCUSSION

1. Before reading *The Why Café*, how would you have answered the three questions on the café menu?— "Why are you here?" "Do you fear death?" "Are you fulfilled?" After having finished the book, would your answers still be the same? If not, why?

2. How pervasive do you think is the feeling Strelecky allegorizes as being lost at night "on a dark, lonely stretch of road"? (p ix) What might account for this sense of being lost and without direction?

3. Have you had an experience similar to John's at the café? If so, how did it change your life and the lives of those close to you?

4. Casey remarks that "sometimes it helps to look at things from a different perspective." (p 33) What might be the benefits of adopting a new perspective? How has looking at things from a different perspective helped you or changed your life? To what extent has *The Why Café* helped you look at things from a new perspective?

5. In reference to the question "Why are you here?" Casey tells John, "If you change the question to no longer be something you ask someone else, but instead you change it to something you ask yourself, you will no longer be the same person." (p 36) What do you think she means by that?

6. In the process of fulfilling one's Purpose For Existing (PFE), what is the importance of exploration and exposure to new ideas and activities?

7. Casey tells John that "we are all limited by our current experiences and knowledge." (p 55) In what ways and to what extent are you limited by your present experience and knowledge? To what degree do we impose those limitations on ourselves?

8. In terms of Casey's story of the green sea turtle and John's reaction to it, what "incoming wave items" are occupying your time and energy every

day? (p 63) How might you cease battling against those "incoming waves" and preserve your energy to take advantage of the "outgoing waves"?

9. Anne remarks to John, "Part of the answer to your question about why we spend so much time preparing to do what we want, instead of just doing it, lies in the messages that are placed in front of us every day." (pp 74–75) How might television, newspapers, magazines, and the Internet affect our daily use of time at our disposal?

10. John questions, "How much of my definition of success, happiness, and fulfillment had been determined by people other than myself?" (p 86) How would you answer this question as it applies to yourself? What actions might you take to change things?

11. At one point, John asks Casey, "Why wait to do what you want, when you can do it right now?" (p 92) How would you respond to that query?

12. What characteristics are shared by people you know who are passionate about what they are doing? Are they the same characteristics that John describes to Casey on page 97?

13. How might "letting people know about something you are trying to do that will help fulfill your PFE"

(p 101) increase your chances of receiving un-expected help and support?

14. John asks Mike, "Why doesn't everyone go after their PFE? What is it that holds them back?" (p 105) How does Mike answer the question? How would you respond?

15. How would you answer the question "Why am I here?" and define *your* Purpose For Existing? How would you go about identifying the activities that will fulfill your PFE?

16. Just before John leaves the café, Casey hands him a menu on which she has written a message for him. What do you think Casey's message is? (p 125) What would you have written to John if you were Casey?

17. In the Epilogue, John remarks, "When you weigh two choices, and one is living a life that fulfills your Purpose For Existing, and the other is just living, you would think the decision is simple. It isn't." Why do you think the decision is not simple? Why do you think that "this is the place where most people end their journey"? (p 127)